SUGAR FLOWERS
& ARRANGEMENTS

LESLEY HERBERT

CONSULTANT · LINDSAY JOHN BRADSHAW

MEREHURST

I dedicate this book to my family, especially my sister Susan and brother Paul, for all their help and support.

≈

Published in 1992 by Merehurst Limited, Ferry House,
51-57 Lacy Road, Putney, London SW15 1PR

ISBN 1-85391-254-9

Managing Editor Katie Swallow
Edited by Jenni Fleetwood
Designed by Peter Bridgewater
Photography by Clive Streeter
Colour Separation by Fotographics Ltd, U.K. - Hong Kong
Printed by Wing King Tong Ltd, Hong Kong

The author and publisher would like to thank the following, many of whom offer a mail order service, for their assistance:

Guy Paul, Unit B4, A1 Industrial Park, Little Socon, Eaton Socon, Cambs, PE19 3JH; Orchard Products, 49 Langdale Road, Hove, E. Sussex, BN3 4HR; PME (Harrow) Ltd, Sugarcraft Division, Brember Road, S. Harrow, Middx, HA2 8UN; Twins Wedding Shop, 67/69 Victoria Road, Romford, Essex, RM1 2LT; J.F. Renshaws Ltd, Mitcham House, River Court, Albert Drive, Woking, Surrey, GU21 5RP; Cel Cakes, Springfield House, Gate Helmsley, York, YO4 1NF; Rainbow Ribbons, Unit D5, Romford Seedbed Centre, Davidson Way, Romford, Essex, RM7 0AZ; Squires Kitchen, 3 Waverley Lane, Farnham, Surrey, GU9 8BB.

NOTES ON USING THE RECIPES

For all recipes, quantities are given in metric, Imperial and cup measurements. Follow one set of measures only as they are not interchangeable. Standard 5ml teaspoons (tsp) and 15ml tablespoons (tbsp) are used. Australian readers, whose tablespoons measure 20ml, should adjust quantities accordingly.
All spoon measures are assumed to be level unless otherwise stated.
Ovens should be pre–heated to specified temperatures.
Microwave oven timings are based on a 650 watt output.
Eggs are a standard size 3 unless otherwise stated.

CONTENTS

INTRODUCTION

*L*esley Herbert's first book in the **Sugarcraft Skills** Series – Bas Relief & Appliqué – has proved a resounding success, and this exquisite guide to sugar flowers is bound to follow suit. There is something deeply satisfying about making these beautiful blooms, and the good news is that the skill is not difficult to acquire. Throughout this book you will find step–by–step instructions, full colour photographs, templates and even diagrams of the suitable cutters to make the task as straightforward as possible. Techniques that help to create realistic results are explained in detail, and Lesley willingly shares the expertise that has made her an acknowledged leader in the field: the lovely wedding cake photographed on page 51 was recently adjudged best in the show (Grand Prix d'Honneur) at the biennial Hotelympia, London. One of the sprays of roses used on that cake is illustrated opposite.

More than a dozen varieties of flower are described, from simple cutter primroses and blossoms to roses, lilies and orchids worthy of the finest corsage. Instructions for making berries, cones and leaves of all types are also included, and there is a section on flower centres and stamens. Lesley stresses the importance of colour in arranging flowers for cakes, and discusses colour theory and the use of the colour wheel.

The latter part of the book concentrates on posies, sprays and bouquets, with comprehensive instructions on wiring flowers, creating the correct balance – even making and using ribbon loops. Designs for special occasion cakes, from a Christening to a Ruby Wedding, appear throughout the book. In every case, the flowers have been carefully chosen to complement the design and occasion. Many of the bouquets or posies can be removed to be kept as keepsakes.

*A*dvanced sugarcraft artists will already have much of the equipment required for flower work, but there are obviously some items peculiar to this skill. The array of *cutters* available can be bewildering; for this reason we have provided templates throughout the book for at–a–glance identification of precisely which cutter is required for any given task. Step pictures also help to clarify the position. *Veiners* are essential, but you can make your own, following the instructions on page 46. Some *stamens* can also be made at home, see page 19, but you will also need a selection of bought stamens. More information on stamens is given on page 18. *Floristry tape* is used constantly. Three types are available; the first is a plastic stretchy film, available in most colours, including pastel tints. It is not the easiest tape to use, but produces a very delicate binding. A paper-type tape is easier to use but can give a thick appearance to stems on flower sprays. There is also a thin plastic tape which is easy to use, but which is not sold in a range of colours. The best approach is to try several types and select the one you find easiest to use. *Covered wire* is available in a selection of gauges; the higher the number (32 gauge),the softer and more pliable the wire. For large flowers or petals, 24 gauge is generally used. *Silver wire* comes in a variety of gauges, either as cut lengths or reels. The reels of wire are useful for binding sprays and bouquets.

Some of the more useful items for flower work,
illustrated opposite, are (clockwise from left):

white and green floristry tape; stamens; cotton (thread); veiners;
Non–toxic modelling clay; non–stick board and rolling pin; posy holders;
cocktail sticks (toothpicks); piping tube (tip); dusting powder (petal dust/blossom tint);
edible food colour pens; brushes; varnish; spray vegetable fat; white non–stick pad;
variety of cutters; foam sponge; yellow non–stick pad; pins; reel wire;
covered wire in various gauges; wooden dowel; bone tool; veining tool; scalpel; scriber;
modelling tools – ball, needle, shell and umbrella; scissors;
palette and cranked palette knives; tweezers; pliers.

To make the cakes illustrated in this book you will also require
greaseproof paper (parchment); wax paper; thin card for templates; ribbons;
Garrett frill cutters; crimpers; dividers and smoothers.

Dried gypsophila is used on some of the sprays and bouquets.

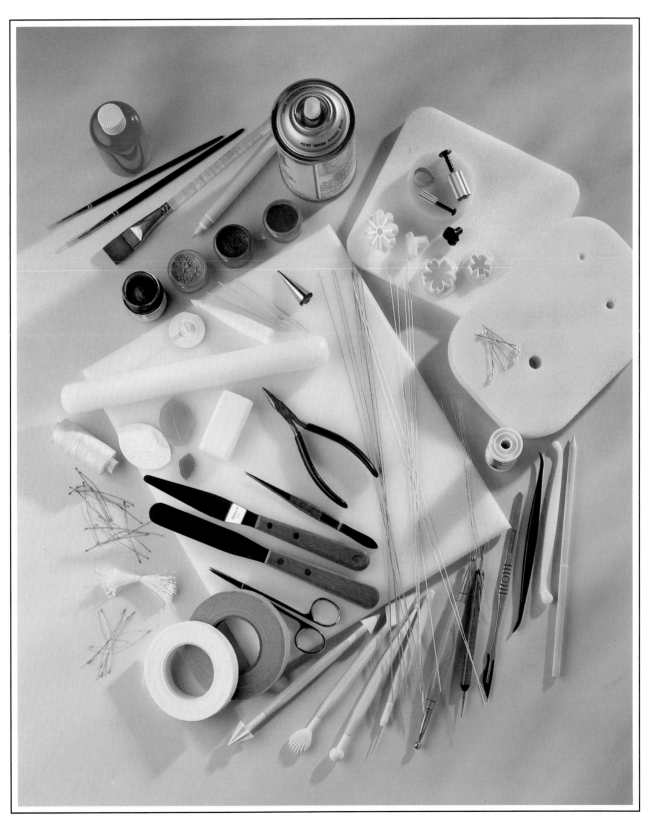

ROYAL ICING

❖

The easiest way to make perfect royal icing is by using the weight ratio 1:6 for egg white and sugar. It is for this reason that a solid measure is given for egg white in the recipe that follows.

125g (4 oz/³/₄ cup) egg white
750g (1¹/₂ lb/4¹/₂ cups) icing (confectioners')
sugar, sifted

● Put egg white in a grease–free bowl. Add three quarters of the icing (confectioners') sugar and beat with an electric mixer for 2 minutes on slow speed. Adjust consistency with remaining sugar and beat for 3 minutes more on slow speed until the icing forms firm peaks. The surface should be glossy; too much icing sugar will result in a matt, grainy appearance. Cover bowl with a damp cloth to prevent icing drying and forming a crust. Makes about 750g (1¹/₂ lb).
NOTE Powdered albumen may be used. Reconstitute it in the proportion of 90g (3 oz/¹/₃ cup) to 625ml (1 pint/2¹/₂ cups) water.

FLOWER PASTE

❖

500g (1 lb/ 3 cups) icing (confectioners') sugar
1 sheet leaf gelatine
2 tsp white vegetable fat (shortening)
2 tsp liquid glucose
1 tsp gum tragacanth
4 tsp CMC (high viscosity
carboxymethyl–cellulose)
1–1¹/₂ egg whites

● Put icing (confectioners') sugar in a heatproof bowl, covering surface closely with greaseproof paper (parchment) to prevent formation of a crust. Warm in a 150°C (300°F/Gas 2) oven.
● Meanwhile soak gelatine in a large bowl of cold water for about 5 minutes until pliable. Remove gelatine from water and place in a small heatproof bowl with fat and glucose. Stand bowl over a saucepan of hot (not boiling) water and stir until contents have dissolved. Mix warmed icing sugar, gum tragacanth and CMC in the warm, dry bowl of a food mixer. Add 1 egg white, with gelatine mixture. Begin mixing at slow speed. Increase mixer speed and beat until paste is white and pliable, adding more egg white if necessary. Store in a clean polythene bag in an airtight container for 24 hours before use, or freeze a portion for future use. Makes about 500g (1 lb).
NOTE If using a small food mixer or hand–held electric mixer, use only half the icing (confectioners') sugar at the mixing stage. The remaining sugar can be kneaded into the paste as it is used. The disadvantage of this method is that it is very time–consuming.

BASIC TECHNIQUES

❖

For successful flower work, it is important to master a few basic techniques. Four of these – frilling, smoothing, cupping and veining – are illustrated and explained opposite. In the pages that follow, more complicated procedures are discussed, with step–by–step photographs to take the mystery out of this beautiful craft.

~ ❖ ~

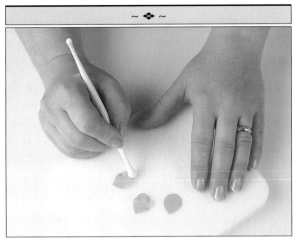

FRILLING *Place ball or bone tool over edge of petal. Rub gently with a back–and–forward motion. Petal edge should form a delicate frill. If the petal cups, move modelling tool a little further from petal edge.*

~ ❖ ~

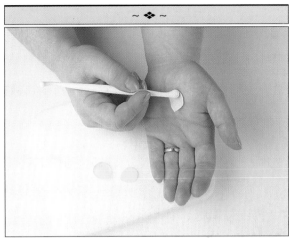

SMOOTHING *Place flower or leaf on the palm of your hand. Place bone tool on edge of petal and gently rub edge. The aim is not to frill the petal, but to soften the appearance of the flower, preventing the cut edge from appearing thick or heavy.*

~ ❖ ~

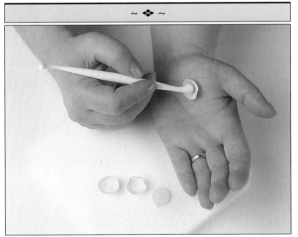

CUPPING *Place petal on the palm of your hand, near the thumb. Using a ball or bone tool, rub centre with a circular motion. If paste has a tendency to stick to hot hands, try cupping petals on the back of your hand, see Step 2, page 23.*

~ ❖ ~

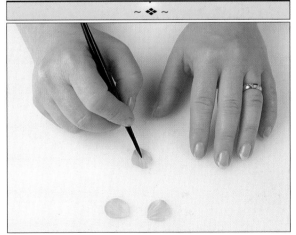

MARKING *Place flower petal or leaf on a non–stick board. Using either end of a veining tool, draw lines from base to edge of petal. Do not apply too much pressure to veining tool or it may cut through paste.*

CUTTER FLOWERS

*T*he easiest way to make flowers is by using one of the many types of cutter available. This technique is used in various ways on the cakes throughout the book, and is particularly suitable for small blooms which become very fragile once dry.

Flower paste, see page 8, is used for all the cutter flowers. Only use a small ball of paste at a time, rolling it out thinly. Thick paste is difficult to frill or cup and the finished flowers may look clumsy.

Step–by–step instructions for making simple cutter flowers – blossom, daphne and primrose – are given opposite. If you are unfamiliar with flower work, read the Expert Advice below.

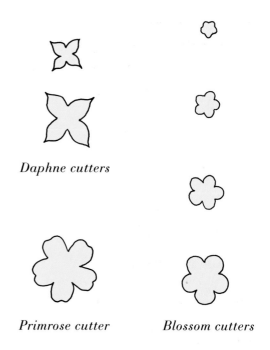

Daphne cutters

Primrose cutter   *Blossom cutters*

EXPERT ADVICE

≈

To make flowers successfully it is essential to have flower paste of the correct consistency. It should be pliable without being sticky. Below are some common problems – and suggested solutions.

● The paste may be very hard, and may crumble when kneaded. If this occurs keep kneading; it will eventually form a solid mass. When it does so, add a little egg white and continue to knead until the desired consistency is achieved.

● The paste may be soft and sticky; it may be difficult to remove from the polythene bag. The solution is to knead in extra icing (confectioners') sugar or cornflour (cornstarch).

● If the paste is short and has no stretch after being kneaded, add a pinch of CMC (carboxymethylcellulose), knead well and place in a polythene bag for 30 minutes before use.

● The paste may dry or the petals crack before modelling is complete. If this happens, add a little white vegetable fat to help slow down the rate at which the paste sets.

● If the cutter flowers stick to the board when being cut, try turning the rolled out paste over briefly before turning it over again. This allows the paste to dry slightly. Keep any unused paste covered with polythene.

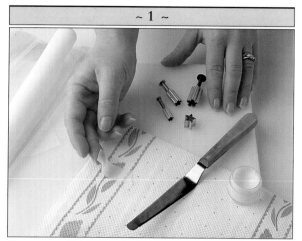

~ 1 ~

BLOSSOM, DAPHNE & PRIMROSE Thinly roll out a small piece of flower paste on a lightly greased non–stick board. Cut out flowers and place on a piece of sponge. Keep remaining paste covered to prevent drying.

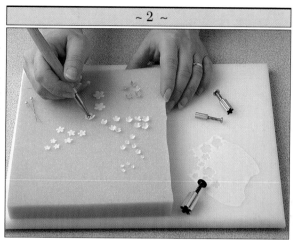

~ 2 ~

Shape flowers on sponge: Place a ball tool on centre of each flower and apply gentle pressure. Use a needle tool or hat pin to make a small hole in middle of each flower. Leave to dry.

~ 3 ~

Thread a stamen through each flower and secure it in place by piping a dot of royal icing in centre of flower. Alternatively, pipe shells in green icing radiating from back of stamen to form a small calyx.

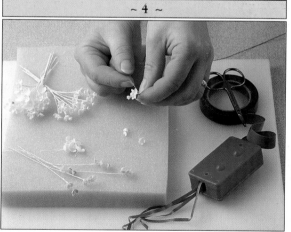

~ 4 ~

Cut or shred some floristry tape into thin strips. Tape 3 or 4 flowers to a piece of 28 gauge wire, keeping the flowers close together. The flowers can be made with coloured paste or brushed with dusting powder when dry.

PULLED FLOWERS

*A*s the name suggests, pulled flowers are made by moulding a basic shape and then stretching or pulling the paste to give the petals form and movement. By altering the shape of the petals, or adding texture as illustrated opposite, the technique can be used for a wide variety of small blooms. The procedure is illustrated in the step–by–step sketches on the right. To wire a pulled flower, make a hook in a 28 gauge wire and thread it through the centre of the flower until the hook is no longer visible.

EXPERT ADVICE

≈

When making pulled flowers, it is important to have all petals the same width and length. Judging where to make the cuts in the flower paste is quite tricky at first, and it is a good idea to practise by making simpler four–petal flowers first.

Take a small ball of paste and mould it into a long, thin teardrop shape.

Dip the point of a dowel in vegetable fat. Holding paste firmly, push dowel 5mm ($1/4$ in) into rounded end of paste.

Remove paste from dowel and cut 5 slits, 5mm ($1/4$ in) long. Open out petals with a fingertip.

Gently pinch just the tip of each petal together to give petals a rounded appearance.

With thumb and index finger, squash each petal flat. This is a basic pulled flower.

TEXTURING PETALS *Cover your index finger with polythene. Hold flower between finger and thumb. Place pointed end of veining tool near centre of petal and press down lightly to indent petal. Do not pull point along petal or petal will be mis–shapen.*

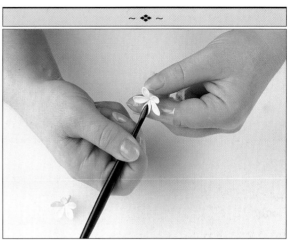

For a different effect, indent the flat end of a veining tool firmly on each petal. Using polythene over your finger prevents the flower from sticking to your skin and the petals from being pulled off.

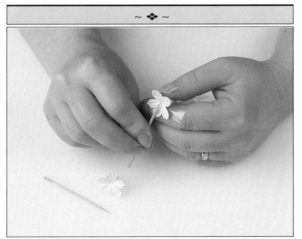

Another method of texturing is to hold the flower between thumb and index finger and press a cocktail stick (toothpick) firmly three times on each petal.

A cocktail stick (toothpick) is also used to thin petals. Roll it gently over the edge of each petal, trying to prevent the point of the stick from damaging the centre of the flower.

CHRISTENING CAKE

18cm (7 in) round cake
apricot glaze
750g (1½ lb) marzipan (almond paste)
clear alcohol (gin or vodka)
1.25kg (2½ lb) sugarpaste
Royal Icing, see page 8
blue, silver and lemon food colourings
glycerol (glycerine), see method

E Q U I P M E N T
25cm (10 in) round cake board
scriber
no. 2, 1, 44 and 42 piping tubes (tips)
wax paper
small paintbrushes
cranked palette knife
1m (1 yd 3 in) lace to trim board
7 white ribbon loops, 5mm (¼ in) wide,
see page 16
5 lemon ribbon loops, 3mm (⅛ in) wide,
see page 16

F L O W E R S
9 sprays white blossom, see page 11
7 sprays blue daphne, see page 11
5 sprays yellow primrose, see page 11

● To obtain correct shape for cake, draw around cake tin (pan) on a sheet of cartridge paper, then re-position tin over front edge and draw an arc. Cut out template and cut cake to shape. Reserve template.

● Brush cake with apricot glaze and cover with marzipan (almond paste). Allow to dry. Brush with clear alcohol. Coat cake and board with sugarpaste, smoothing surfaces. When coating is firm, place cake on board. Trace name of infant on reserved template. Centre template on top of cake, making sure name is straight.

Scribe name.

● With template still in position as guide for line work, pipe small S- and C-scrolls in white royal icing with a no. 2 tube (tip), leaving a 1cm (½ in) space between scrolls. Remove template. Using blue royal icing and a no. 1 tube, pipe a dot flower between each scroll. Soften some blue royal icing and run out name directly on top of cake, see Note, page 16. Dry.

● Make stork. Trace template below. Cover tracing with wax paper, then pipe outline, using a no. 2 tube (tip) and white royal icing, Use a damp paintbrush to smooth any joins. When dry, overpipe outline with the same tube.

Continued on page 16

Continued from page 14

● When icing is perfectly dry, remove stork from paper by carefully sliding a cranked palette knife between paper and figure. Paint stork with silver food colouring, allow it to dry, then turn over and paint reverse side.

● Add a small amount of glycerol (glycerine) to some white royal icing to prevent it from becoming hard and brittle. Using this icing and a no. 44 tube (tip), pipe a shell border around base of cake. Using same icing but a no. 42 tube, overpipe shells, following diagram below.

● Cut a 'V' in the pointed end of a paper piping bag, fill it with softened white royal icing and pipe a wing on each swan. Using a no. 1 tube (tip) pipe 2 lines on each beak. Finally, pipe eyes, using blue royal icing and a no. 1 tube.

● Trim board with lace. Using sprays of flowers and ribbon loops make up a small direct flower spray on the sugarpaste–covered board to fill cut out portion of cake, see page 61.

● With the end of a paintbrush, make a hole in the sugarpaste on the board. Fill hole with royal icing, then carefully position stork. Do not push down hard on legs as they are fragile. Allow icing to dry before transporting cake.

NOTE Detailed instructions for runouts are not included as the technique is covered elsewhere in the *Sugarcraft Skills* Series.

~ 1 ~

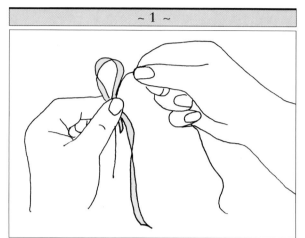

RIBBON LOOPS Make a loop at one end of a length of ribbon. Hold loop between finger and thumb of left hand, with long end of ribbon trailing. Pinch a piece of 28 gauge wire between same finger and thumb, holding free end with right hand.

~ 4 ~

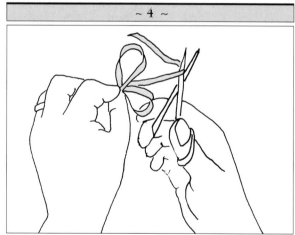

Cut ribbon at an angle to prevent fraying. A long tail may be left if required.

~ 2 ~

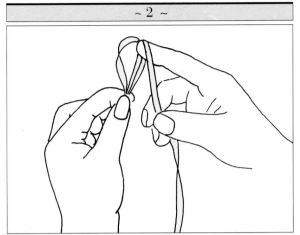

Tightly wrap wire twice around ribbon loop. Holding wire–bound ribbon firmly, make a second loop from trailing end of ribbon, using index finger as a guide.

~ 3 ~

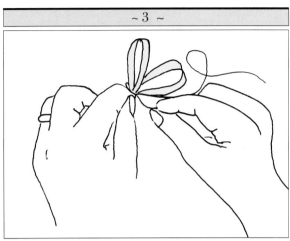

Twist wire around second ribbon loop, just below previous wire binding.

~ 5 ~

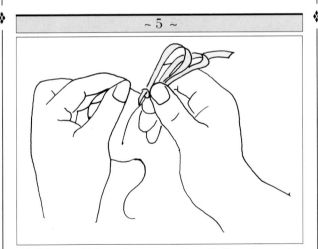

Holding ribbon loops and tail firmly, twist wires together.

~ 6 ~

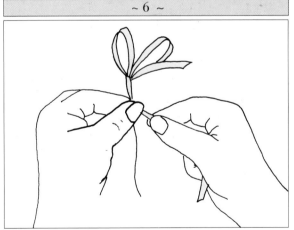

Bind end of ribbon and wires, using a thin strip of floristry tape. This method of making ribbon loops has a neat small back. If required, extra ribbon loops can be made, with each binding wire slightly below the last.

FLOWER CENTRES

A variety of techniques can be used to make flower centres, from simple dots of royal icing on cutter flowers to delicate cotton stamens. The secret, as with other aspects of this craft, is to imitate nature as closely as possible. Study the real flower – or a good photograph or botanical drawing – and make the centre accordingly.

STAMENS

A wide variety of colours and sizes is available, from white stamens which can be tinted by dipping in a solution of food colouring to jet black stamens for anemones and similar flowers. Matt or pearl heads look attractive in cutter flowers, the tiny heads lending themselves particularly well to apple blossom. Stamens are usually sold in bunches of 144 heads.

The finest and most delicate stamens are *Japanese stamens*. These look very realistic when used with small blooms, but are rather difficult to handle.

Stiff stamens can easily be placed into the throat of a flower, but soft ones may need to be taped on wires.

Cotton stamens, used principally for roses, are generally coloured after being cut: dip the ends of the cotton (thread) in white vegetable fat, then in fine cornmeal or semolina which has been coloured with dusting powder (petal dust/blossom tint).

EXPERT ADVICE

≈

To create a small orchid, make a pulled flower as described on page 12. Using the cutter sketched below, cut out the orchid throat. Frill the scalloped edge of the throat with a cocktail stick (toothpick), then complete the flower, following the instructions opposite. If preferred, a pulled cutter flower (page 26) may be used.

Orchid throat cutter

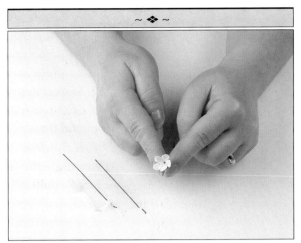

STAMENS *Tape 5 stamens to a piece of 28 gauge wire. Bend tip of wire into a hook over tape, then insert wire through flower until hook is embedded in flower centre. Secure paste firmly by working back of flower between index fingers.*

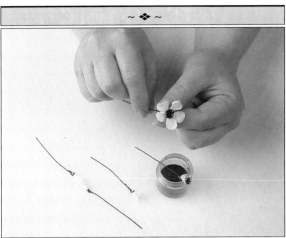

COTTON STAMENS *Wind cotton around index finger. Twist 28 gauge wire tightly through each side of loop, binding wire around back to make cotton stand up. Cut cotton in half; colour as described opposite. See also Step 1, page 49.*

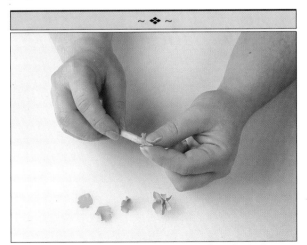

ORCHID *Paint egg white on 'V' of orchid throat, see Expert Advice opposite. Wrap paste around dowel point to make a cone, with 'V' just overlapping. When dry, paint egg white in flower centre; Insert orchid throat. See also page 59.*

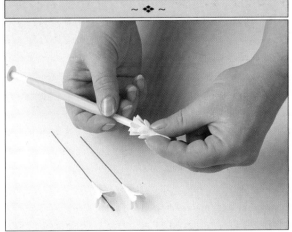

TEXTURED CENTRE *Hold a lightly greased modelling tool in flower centre while gently pinching back of flower with other hand. Remove modelling tool and insert a piece of 28 gauge wire until tiny hook is embedded in flower centre.*

FIGURE OF EIGHT RIBBON LOOPS

*T*his method of making ribbons is useful when making posies as it can be used in place of the first row of flowers to give a basic outline.

Make a loop of ribbon, holding it between index finger and thumb.

Bring ribbon round to form a figure of eight, holding centre. Repeat to form a second figure of eight.

Fold a piece of 28 gauge wire in half to resemble a hairpin. Place over centre of ribbons where they cross.

Pull the 4 loops together, adjusting centre to ensure loops are the same length; twist wire together as close to ribbon as possible.

Open out bow. The twisted loops should look like a double figure of eight, with the twisted wire at the back.

ARUM LILY

*A*rum lilies are once again fashionable for weddings. Although they are very large blooms, they can be made in miniature to provide useful filler flowers. The long slim shape of the lily makes a nice contrast in bouquets and sprays of flowers, especially if several sizes of lily are used. White arums are illustrated here, but there are also pink and yellow varieties.

To make the arum lily, prepare the stamen as described in Step 1 right. Then roll out paste as thinly as possible on a lightly greased board, select cutter of suitable size (see below) and cut out petal. Place petal on sponge pad and smooth edge with a bone tool. Mark a line down centre of petal and dampen bottom straight edge with egg white. Complete flower, following Step 2 right.

Arum lily cutters

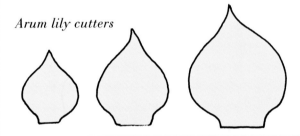

EXPERT ADVICE

≈

An interesting texture to represent pollen on flowers can be made by mixing coloured dusting powder (petal dust/blossom tint) with cornmeal or semolina. This has been used for the arum lilies opposite, as well as for the cutter blossom on page 11 and open rose centres on page 49.

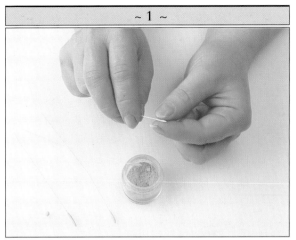

Make stamen by rolling a tiny piece of yellow paste onto the top of a length of 28 gauge wire; paste should be same length as cutter being used. Dip paste into egg white and then into yellow cornmeal. Allow to dry.

Place prepared stamen on one side of arum lily petal. Roll petal around wire. Pinch tip of lily; gently pull back. Slightly curl back outer edge of flower so that it appears to be opening.

VIOLET

*U*sing a suitable cutter, as shown right, cut out five petals from violet coloured paste. Smooth edges of four petals, then frill edge of remaining petal by applying more pressure to ball tool and placing tool on very edge of petal. Cup centres of petals as described on page 9.

Turn two petals over. Brush egg white on edge of first petal, then overlap second petal as in sketch 1 right. Paint egg white on centre point of this pair of petals, then position one petal horizontally on either side so that they overlap the centre points, see sketch 2. Place the final petal in the centre, at the position where all the other petal points meet. Allow violet to dry before painting small white lines on the petals, radiating from the centre. Finally, dab a little yellow colour in the centre.

CHRISTMAS ROSE

*T*his starts off in much the same way as the apple blossom opposite. Using a suitable cutter, as shown right, cut out a calyx from green paste. Place the calyx in a hoop, see Step 1, opposite. Roll out some white paste as thinly as possible and cut out five petals. Frill their edges, then cup their centres with a ball tool.

To assemble the roses, brush egg white on the calyx, then add the petals, overlapping them on the calyx as shown in the sketch right. Pipe a dot of yellow royal icing in the centre of the flower and add lots of small dots around the centre to represent stamens. Artificial stamens can be used instead, but the flower will not be edible.

Violet cutter

1. *Overlapping centre petals*

2. *Adding horizontal outer petals*

Christmas rose

Calyx cutter

Petal cutter/make 5

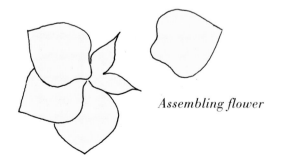

Assembling flower

~ 1 ~

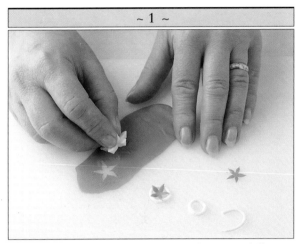

APPLE BLOSSOM Mould some hoops of flower paste for supporting blossom; leave to dry. Roll out green paste on a lightly greased board. Cut out small calyx, gently cup centre with ball tool, then place over hoop to dry.

~ 2 ~

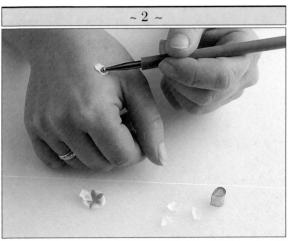

Roll out small amount of white or pastel paste as thinly as possible (you should be able to read print through the paste). Cut out 5 small petals. Frill edges with a ball tool, then cup centres, working on back of hand if paste tends to stick.

~ 3 ~

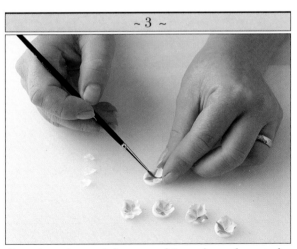

Brush calyx with egg white. Attach petals, overlapping them on calyx. The first petal may need to be lifted slightly to enable final petal to be inserted, thus completing spiral effect.

~ 4 ~

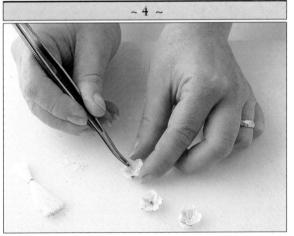

While petals are still pliable use tweezers to insert as many tiny stamens around centre of blossom as possible. Place tiny ball of green paste in middle. Accentuate petal edges by brushing with pink dusting powder.

HAPPY BIRTHDAY

This cake can be used for any occasion, simply by changing the picture. The benefit of painting on a runout plaque is that several attempts can be made and the best one used for the cake.

28 x 20cm (11 x 8 in) elongated
octagonal cake
apricot glaze
1.5kg (3 lb) marzipan (almond paste)
clear alcohol (gin or vodka)
1.5kg (3 lb) sugarpaste
small amount of Royal Icing, see page 8
selection of food colourings
EQUIPMENT
36 x 28cm (14 x 11 in) elongated
octagonal cake board
no. 2, 1 and 0 piping tubes (tips)
wax paper
scriber
fine paintbrushes
FLOWERS
22 apple blossom, see page 23
38 small rose leaves, see page 45
75 cutter blossom – in shades of blue, violet and
heather, see page 11

● Brush cake with apricot glaze and cover with marzipan (almond paste). Brush cake with alcohol. Roll out sugarpaste and coat cake. When dry, secure cake to board with royal icing.

● Make a greaseproof paper (parchment) template for linework on side of cake, following design opposite. Secure template to centre front side of cake with pins. Outline template in white royal icing, using a no. 2 tube (tip). Overpipe line in same icing, but with a no. 1 tube.

● Use same tube and icing to pipe another line on the inside of the overpiped line. Repeat on three remaining main sides of cake. Using same icing but a no. 2 tube, pipe a shell border on cake base.

● Using template on page 69, make a runout plaque on wax paper for top of cake, see Note, page 16. Place plaque in a warm place to dry. Using white royal icing, run out four teddy bears, using template on page 69. Finally run out one bluebird in white icing, see template, page 69.

● When runouts are dry, remove them from wax paper. Trace picture of baby on page 69. Transfer tracing to plaque, then paint all runouts with food colourings, remembering to start with background areas, and adding shading and detail gradually.

● Scribe sprays of flowers and inscription on top of cake, using templates on page 69. Paint small leaves directly on sugarpaste coating. Position painted plaque and secure with royal icing. Pipe inscription with heather coloured royal icing and a no. 0 tube (tip). Secure painted runout teddy bears to four side corner panels. Lastly secure flowers and leaves to top and sides of cake with dots of icing, using photograph opposite as guide; fix tiny bluebird to plaque.

NOTE Detailed instructions for painting on runout plaques are not included in this book as the technique is covered elsewhere in the *Sugarcraft Skills* series.

PULLED CUTTER FLOWERS

*H*aving mastered cutter flowers and pulled flowers, combine the twin skills and move on to making pulled cutter flowers. For this technique the back of the flower is modelled by hand; a cutter is used solely to shape the petals. This method of making flowers is very versatile; most shapes of cutter can be used successfully.

1 Make a small ball of paste into a 'light bulb' shape by gently working paste between index fingers of both hands.

2 Pinch lower part of bulb until shape resembles a Mexican hat.

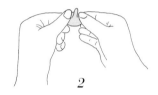

3 Place shaped paste on a lightly greased board and roll out sides as thinly as possible; a dowel or knitting needle is ideal for this purpose.

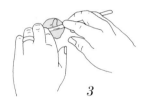

4 Place chosen cutter over paste. Cut out flower, removing excess paste cleanly. Using a knife, lift flower from board.

5 Place point of greased dowel in centre of flower, penetrating about 3mm ($\frac{1}{8}$ in). Gently pull dowel towards your thumb to form the throat. Do not hollow centre too much or flower will not hold on wire. Make a hook in a 28 gauge wire, then insert wire through flower centre until hook buries itself in the flower.

EXPERT ADVICE

≈

Keep the back of the flower small; thick paste may get stuck in the cutter. If the flower does get stuck, release it with a soft paintbrush.

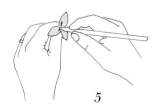

Pulled cutter flowers

PULLED CUTTER BLOSSOM

*U*sing green paste, make a pulled cutter flower and attach it to 28 gauge wire as described opposite. This will form the calyx for the blossom.

Cut out two small circular carnation petals, using a suitable cutter, as illustrated below. Place on a non-stick board and frill the edges, following Step 1 right.

Paint egg white in the centre of the calyx, then place one frilled petal on top. Finish the blossom following Step 2.

Feathered carnation cutters, also used for pulled cutter blossom

Calyx

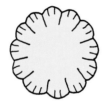

Petal make 2

EXPERT ADVICE

≈

While the icing is still soft, sprinkle a little cornmeal in the centre of the flower to represent pollen. Gently shake off excess. These flowers look very attractive if the edges are dusted with dusting powder (petal dust/blossom tint): Dip a 2cm (³/₄ in) brush in the powder, tap off excess, then brush flower tips from edge to centre.

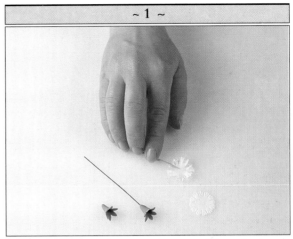

~ 1 ~

Frill edge of each carnation petal by placing a cocktail stick (toothpick) 1cm (¹/₂ in) over edge of paste and rolling stick gently back and forth.

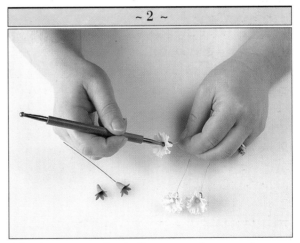

~ 2 ~

Having attached first petal to calyx as described above left, carefully push centre of blossom with a small ball tool. Add second petal in the same way. Allow to dry, then pipe a bulb of yellow royal icing in centre of flower.

LARGE CARNATION

*U*sing green paste and the cutter illustrated below, make a pulled cutter flower as described on page 26. This will form the calyx for the large carnation. Having cut out the calyx and removed excess paste, lift it from the board. Place the point of a greased dowel in the centre of the calyx, penetrating about 3mm (1/8 in). Lift petals towards dowel, then hollow centre and texture outside of calyx, following Step 1 right. Set calyx aside to dry. Then add petals, following steps 2–3.

Large carnation cutters

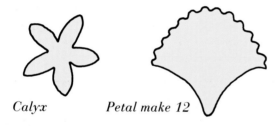

Calyx   *Petal make 12*

FEATHERED CARNATION

*C*ut out 2 round carnation petals using the cutter shown on page 27. It is not necessary to cut a calyx. Frill both petals by rolling a cocktail stick (toothpick) around the edge, then proceed as described in Steps 1 and 2 opposite. Having completed the 'Z' fold, pinch the base of the flower to secure the paste firmly to the wire. Allow to dry, then add the second petal as described in Step 3. When the feathered carnation is complete, allow it to dry completely before dusting the edges with dusting powder (petal dust/blossom tint).

~ 1 ~

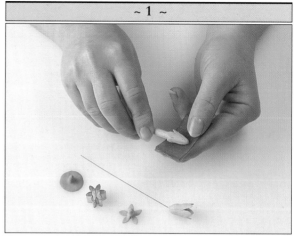

LARGE CARNATION Holding calyx on dowel, gently roll over crepe paper or veiner. Make a small hook in a 26 gauge wire; bend hook over to golf club shape. Push wire through calyx, then secure by covering hook with a tiny ball of green paste. Dry.

~ 1 ~

FEATHERED CARNATION Paint egg white on the centre of one of the carnation petals, then carefully insert a hooked 28 gauge wire through centre of paste.

~ 2 ~

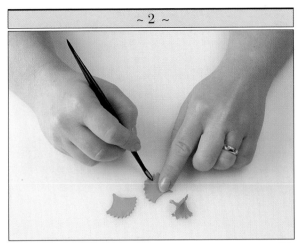

Using cutter illustrated opposite, cut out 12 carnation petals. Frill curved edge of each petal by pulling flat edge of veining tool over petal edge onto non-stick board. Fold petal slightly.

~ 3 ~

Brush egg white on inside of calyx. Place petals around edge, keeping ends of petals damp with egg white and pressing petals onto calyx with veining tool. Continue adding petals until calyx is full. Allow to dry.

~ 2 ~

Fold petal in half. Paint egg white on centre, then fold one third of petal forward. Turn petal over. Paint egg white on centre, then fold one third back to make a 'Z' fold with wire firmly held in the middle of the flower.

~ 3 ~

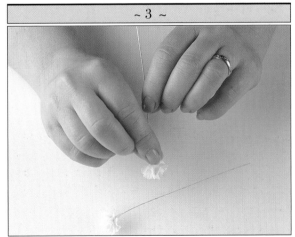

Paint egg white on centre of second frilled petal and carefully push onto wire behind folded petal. Turn flower upside down and gently pinch paste around back of flower. Allow carnation to dry.

FREESIA

*F*reesias and daffodils (page 35) are made by the combination method. A cutter is used to make part of each flower, but the pulled cutter technique is also utilized.

A freesia is made up of two layers, each consisting of a set of three petals. Using a suitable cutter, as shown right, cut out a three-petal shape from cream coloured paste. Use the same paste for a second three petal shape, this time using the pulled cutter method described on page 26. Tape four stamens, one slightly longer than the rest, to a 26 gauge wire, then shape the flower, following Steps 1–3 opposite.

To complete the freesia, cut two petals from green paste, using the edge of the cutter. Smooth the edges of the green petals and secure one on each side of the bottom of the flower. Colour the back stem and inside throat of the flower with yellow dusting powder (petal dust/blossom tint).

To make a bud, thread a small ball of green paste onto a 28 gauge hooked wire. Roll the top of the paste gently between the index finger and thumb until the hook is buried. Roll the bottom of paste to a long teardrop shape. Allow to dry. Make about 6 buds of varying sizes and tones of green for each spray of freesia; the smaller the bud the deeper the colour. Add two green petals to each bud as for the flower. A single spray of freesias is shown in Step 3 opposite, while the final photograph shows freesias in combination with carnations, daphne and blossom on the Engagement Cake.

Freesia petal cutter

EXPERT ADVICE

≈

Select flower cutters with care. They should have sharp cutting edges and should not buckle when pressed. Metal, nickel silver and plastic cutters are available, some with guards to protect the hands from being marked. Throughout this book you will find sketches of the ideal cutters to use for specific types of flowers. If you are unable to find the correct cutter, you can make a card template and cut around it, but the paste may drag, spoiling the definition of the petal or leaf.

~ 1 ~

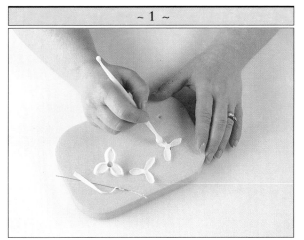

FREESIA Insert back of pulled cutter flower into hole in pad. Cup all petals, using a bone tool. If unsure of technique, see page 9. Brush egg white on centre of pulled cutter flower. Add cut out set of petals to make a 6–petal flower.

~ 2 ~

Lightly grease point of dowel and insert 3mm (¹/₈ in) into centre of flower. Starting with inner set, bring petals in towards dowel to make two layers. Gently pinch back of paste; remove from dowel.

~ 3 ~

Insert wire with prepared stamens. Rub stem between index fingers to form a long tapered back, removing excess paste if necessary. Hang flower upside down to dry, then finish as described opposite. Make buds; combine with flowers in spray.

~ 4 ~

Sprays of freesias look very effective with more formal flowers such as carnations, see page 28.

ENGAGEMENT CAKE

25 x 20cm (10 x 8 in) oval cake
apricot glaze
1.25kg (2¹/₂ lb) marzipan (almond paste)
1.5kg (3 lb) Royal Icing, see page 8
blue, peach and green food colourings
6 large and 6 small unwired peach blossom,
see page 11
posy, see page 34
EQUIPMENT
33 x 28cm (13 x 11 in) oval cake board
wax paper
no. 1, 2 and 42 piping tubes (tips)
perspex (plexiglass) vase
2 figures for top of cake, optional
ribbon to trim board

Brush cake with apricot glaze and cover with marzipan and white royal icing. Coat cake board with royal icing, applying several coats to obtain a good surface. Allow to dry.

Using templates on page 70, run out 6 oval plaques and 6 hollow hearts on wax paper, see Note, page 16. Make 6 tracings of each pair of birds and each pair of wings on page 70. Cover with wax paper. Using a no.1 tube (tip) and blue royal icing, pipe all the individual wings. When wings are quite dry, pipe all the birds' bodies. While icing is still soft position wings on birds. When birds are dry, remove them from wax paper and fix them to prepared oval plaques.

Measure height and circumference of cake and make a greaseproof paper (parchment) template. Fold template into 6 equal sections and cut scalloped design, see page 70. Attach paper template to side of cake, securing ends with masking tape.

Make paper template of cake board, indicating position of cake by drawing around cake tin (pan). Draw design for scallops on board, corresponding to those on side of cake; in effect shadowing side design. Cut out template; place on coated cake board.

Graduated line work, using white royal icing and a no. 1 tube (tip) only, is used on both board and side of cake. Each design consists of 3 layers, 2 layers and a single layer of line piping. Complete line work on board first, piping around template. Remove template, then secure cake to board, using a small amount of royal icing. Fill any gaps between cake and board with icing before piping a small shell border around base of cake with a no. 2 tube. Allow board line work and border to dry.

Using exactly the same method as for the board, pipe graduated line work around template on side of cake.

Secure large peach blossoms on board between scallops before attaching run–out hearts. Attach prepared oval plaques, decorating top of each oval with a single small peach blossom and small piped green icing shells to represent leaves. Complete side design by piping a bow shape between plaques. Divide top edge of cake into 12 equal sections. Using a no. 42 tube (tip) and full peak royal icing, pipe S–scrolls. Overpipe with same tube, then use a no.2 tube.

Make the posy, following the step–by–step instructions on page 34. Display it in the vase on top of the cake. Add the figures, if using, and complete the cake by trimming the board with ribbon.

~ 1 ~

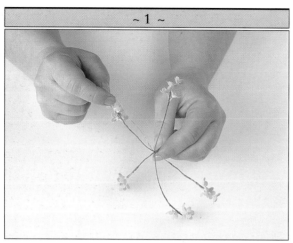

Posy The aim of making a posy is to build all the wired flowers into one stem. Place 5 sprays of peach blossom together, bending wires to 90° to form a circle the size of required posy. Secure top of stems with reel wire (this is the binding point).

~ 2 ~

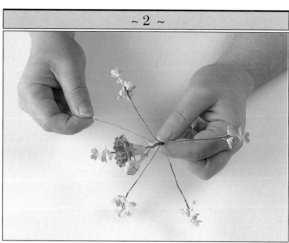

Position focal flower (in this posy, the carnation) in the centre. The height of this flower stem should measure approximately the same as vertical blossom stems. Bind into place.

~ 3 ~

Continue adding rows of flowers: 5 sprays blue daphne, 5 sprays freesia, 5 orange carnations, 5 carnation leaves; 3 extra sprays blue daphne, 3 sprays blossom. Cut some wire out of posy close to binding point to prevent stem becoming too thick.

~ 4 ~

When posy is complete, wind reel wire down stem. Cut stems to required length; bind with white floristry tape to cover all the wire. Figure of eight ribbon loops (page 20), can be taped behind posy if required.

DAFFODIL

*L*ike freesias, daffodils are made by the combination method. Using a suitable cutter, as shown below, cut out the trumpet shape from yellow paste. Complete the trumpet, following Step 1 right.

For the petals, use paste which is a lighter shade of yellow than the trumpet. Using the petal cutter below, cut out two shapes, each consisting of three petals. Place on a non–stick pad and smooth around all the edges with a bone tool.

Brush egg white on the centre of one set of petals and add the second set to make a 6–petal flower. If unsure of technique, see Step 1, page 31. Mark three lines down each petal with the narrow end of a veining tool.

Add the trumpet, following Step 2 opposite. Stamens can be added by dropping a small ball of paste into the trumpet and inserting the stamens with tweezers. However, if the flowers are to be eaten, the stamens should be omitted.

Daffodil petal cutter

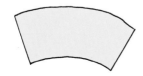

Daffodil trumpet cutter

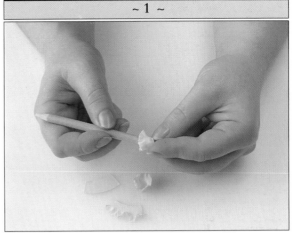

~ 1 ~

Frill widest edge of trumpet shape by rolling a cocktail stick (toothpick) gently along the paste. Paint egg white along one side. Wrap paste around dowel, overlapping egg white side. Carefully pinch bottom of paste to a cone shape.

~ 2 ~

Paint egg white on centre of petals and gently push trumpet into position. Remove dowel very carefully. Add stamens, following instructions left, if liked.

EASTER CAKE

25 x 20cm (10 x 8 in) scalloped oval cake
apricot glaze
1.5kg (3 lb) marzipan (almond paste)
clear alcohol (gin or vodka)
2kg (4 lb) sugarpaste
Royal Icing, see page 8
selection of food colourings

E Q U I P M E N T

33 x 28cm (13 x 11 in) scalloped oval cake
board
scalpel
scriber
no. 2, 1 and 0 piping tubes (tips)
Garrett frill cutter
cocktail stick (toothpick)
paintbrushes
lemon ribbon to trim board
wax paper

F L O W E R S

3 daffodils, see page 35; 3 violets, see page 22;
6 primroses, see page 11; 6 leaves, see page 45

● Brush cake with apricot glaze and cover with marzipan (almond paste). Brush cake top only with alcohol and cover with sugarpaste, leaving sides plain. Smooth sugarpaste to give a rounded edge to top of cake. Dry for two days.

● Brush sides and top edge of cake only with clear alcohol, then coat entire cake with white sugarpaste. Trace oval template on page 68 and cut out of thin but firm card. While cake coating is still soft, place template on cake top. Cut through sugarpaste around template with scalpel. Remove sugarpaste oval, which will not stick to sugarpaste below since no alcohol was brushed there. Use fingertips to smooth cut edge. Coat board with sugarpaste. When coating is dry secure cake to board with a small amount of royal icing.

● Measure height and circumference of cake and make a greaseproof paper (parchment) template. Fold template into four equal sections. Draw a shallow curve for each frill, then trace embroidery design (page 68) above each scallop. Attach paper template to each side of cake in turn; scribe curves and embroidery design.

● Pipe a small shell border around cake base, using white royal icing and a no. 2 tube (tip). Using cutter, lemon sugarpaste and cocktail stick (toothpick) make Garrett frills, see Note. Moisten marked line on cake with a damp brush and quickly attach frills, gently lifting them with a soft dry brush. Neaten top edge of frills with a herringbone shell pattern piped with a no. 1 tube and white royal icing.

● Pipe daffodils for side pattern, using yellow royal icing and a no. 0 tube; for centres pipe three circles on top of each other to form a trumpet. Pipe violet spot flowers between daffodils; paint sprays of leaves. Trim board edge with lemon ribbon.

● Using template on page 68, run out the bunny in white royal icing on wax paper, see Note, page 16. When dry, paint with food colouring to create fur effect.

● Scribe basic outline of top design on cake. Paint daffodil leaves and butterfly with food colourings, then pipe embroidered flowers before attaching runout bunny. Position flowers and leaves before securing them to cake with dots of royal icing.

NOTE Detailed instructions for making the Garrett frills are not included in this book as the technique is covered elsewhere in the *Sugarcraft Skills* Series.

COLOUR

*I*n a book of this type it is not possible to expand at great length on the theory of colour, but it is useful to explore some basic facts about the composition of colour and how best to use it to advantage.

When a beam of light is refracted, it breaks down into seven distinct colours – red, orange, yellow, green, blue, indigo and violet. Three of these colours – red, yellow and blue – are termed *primary colours*. It is from these that all other colours are made. When two primary colours are mixed together, *secondary colours* are produced. Thus blue and yellow are mixed to make green, red and yellow are mixed to create orange and blue and red make violet.

Sugarcraft artists frequently mix colours in this way, and it is interesting to experiment, varying the ratio of one colour to another to produce a variety of secondary hues. The process can be taken further, as when secondary colours are mixed together to produce *tertiary* colours like coffee, olive and rust.

Artists frequently use a colour circle, in which the colours appear in the same order as they do on a rainbow. In the colour circle opposite, the breaking up of the main colours is taken further. From the top, in a clockwise direction, the colours are yellow, orange yellow, orange, red orange, red, red violet, violet, blue violet, blue, green blue, green and yellow green. Yellow is the lightest colour and has the highest value; violet is the darkest hue and has the lowest value.

White, black and their product – grey – are not true colours. When white is added to a colour, as in the inner wheel of the circle opposite, a *tint* is produced and the colour value is increased. Tints are widely used in cake decorating, as when colour is added to white icing or flower paste.

When black is added to a colour, the colour value is decreased, and a *shade* is produced. Shades are shown in the innermost ring of the colour circle. They are not widely used in cake decoration, but it may be useful to add black to green when making foliage colours.

COLOUR SCHEMES

The colour circle can be a great help when planning a scheme for a cake or flower arrangement.

By selecting varying intensities of the same colour a *monochromatic* scheme can be produced, as when pale pink, deep rose, red and burgundy are judiciously used.

Colours which are opposite each other on the colour circle are termed *complementary*; yellow and violet are complementary; so are red and green; orange and blue. To obtain an interesting scheme try using paler or darker tints of the same colour, for instance cream, lemon and yellow, with a small amount of a complementary colour such as violet. In order to make a colour appear more brilliant, it can be surrounded by its complementary colour.

Harmony is achieved when two to four adjacent colours on the colour circle are used together. The colours should not be used full strength or the result would be gaudy. Only one primary colour is used.

Triadic: This is the use of three colours equidistant on the colour circle – for example red, blue and yellow. Colours do not have to be used at full strength or in equal amounts.

SWEET PEA

weet peas are always popular and are particularly appropriate for 'feminine' cakes. Examples of suitable cutters for the various petals are illustrated below.

For a sweet pea bloom, start by making a hook in a 26 gauge wire. Fill hole in hook with flower paste and set aside. Roll out flower paste thinly. Using the appropriate cutter, cut out a rose petal shape for the first petal. Frill the edges as described on page 9 Assemble the basic flower, following Steps 1–3 opposite.

When the sweet pea is dry, make the calyx by cutting out a star shape from green paste. Smooth edges of calyx, paint centre with egg white and thread onto wire, pinching calyx to back of flower. Finally, add tendrils as described in Step 4 opposite.

EXPERT ADVICE

≈

To make a sweet pea bud, use two frilled rose petal shapes. Having attached the first petal as shown in Step 1 opposite, add a second petal in the same way. Allow the petals to dry before adding a calyx as described for full blooms. Buds and flowers can be taped together or used separately in arrangements.

Sweet pea cutters

Calyx

Sweet pea inner petal (1st)

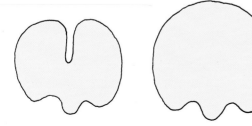

2nd petal   *3rd petal*

~ 1 ~

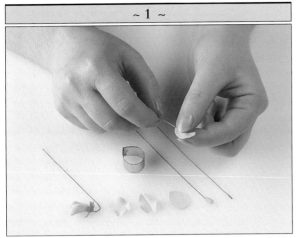

SWEET PEA *Mark a line down the centre of the frilled petal. Paint egg white thinly over the surface. Fold petal in half, enclosing hooked wire.*

~ 2 ~

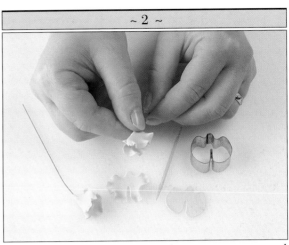

Using cutter shown opposite, cut out second flower petal. Frill outer edge, paint egg white down centre and attach to prepared wire. The folded point of the previous petal should be visible through cut section of second petal.

~ 3 ~

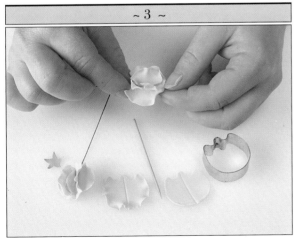

Cut out third petal, using appropriate cutter. Mark centre line with veining tool; frill rounded edge. Paint egg white on each end of marked line and attach to previous petals at stem. Allow to dry.

~ 4 ~

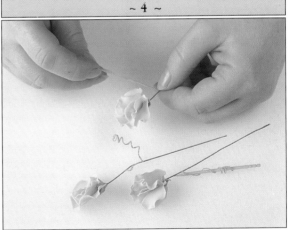

Tendrils are made from a thin strip of floristry tape. Fold tape in half over wire and twist ends together. Wind twisted tape loosely around a cocktail stick (toothpick), then carefully remove, leaving tape curled.

18th BIRTHDAY CAKE

20 cm (8 in) square cake
apricot glaze
1kg (2 lb) marzipan (almond paste)
1.5kg (3 lb) sugarpaste
clear alcohol (gin or vodka)
Royal Icing, see page 8
selection of food colourings
pink lustre and violet dusting powder
(petal dust/blossom tint)

EQUIPMENT

30cm (12 in) cake board
modelling tool
4m (4 1/3 yd) pink ribbon, 3mm (1/8 in) wide
2m (2 yd 6 in) violet ribbon, 3mm (1/8 in) wide
crimper
no. 2 and 1 piping tubes (tips)
1.5cm (1 2/3 yd) pink lace to trim board
green floristry tape for sweet pea tendrils
small posy holder

FLOWERS

8 large blossom, see page 11
22 medium blossom, see page 11
32 small blossom in pink, white and violet, see page 11
3 sweet pea buds, see page 40
9 sweet pea flowers, see page 41

● Place cake on board. Brush with apricot glaze and cover with marzipan (almond paste). Roll a long rope of sugarpaste 1cm (1/2 in) in diameter. Brush marzipanned cake with clear alcohol, place sugarpaste rope around base of cake, then coat cake and board with sugarpaste in one piece.

● Gently push modelling tool into coated rope of sugarpaste. Use most of the ribbon to trim the side of the cake. Stick a length of violet ribbon centrally on the side of the cake, securing it with royal icing, then stick a length of pink ribbon above and below it. Reserve the remaining ribbon for bows. While the cake coating is still soft, crimp above and below the ribbon line as shown in photograph. Allow to dry for three days.

● Enlarge linked numerals on page 70 and carefully cut out a template from firm paper. Place template on cake. Pipe a small shell border around the edge, using pink royal icing and a no. 2 tube (tip). Allow to dry before brushing pink lustre colour inside numerals – a 2cm (3/4 in) chisel paintbrush is ideal for this and helps to achieve uniform colour.

● Scribe name on cake. Run out letters direct, using softened royal icing, see Note on page 16.

● Cut out blossom and gift tag from flower paste, using template on page 70. When tag is dry, pipe 'with love', using violet royal icing and a no.1 tube (tip). Attach small blossom sprays to each corner of board, tag and numerals on cake with dots of royal icing. Pipe a small pink dot in the centre of each blossom.

● Using one length of each colour of remaining ribbon, tie the ribbon bows. Attach to corner of cake with icing. Trim board with lace. Make up a spray, using sweet pea buds and flowers, and adding tendrils as described in Step 4, page 41. Insert posy holder into centre of numeral 8 to accommodate spray of sweet peas.

NOTE For more information on posy holders, see page 60.

LEAVES

Take as much care with leaves as you do with making flowers and your reward will be a natural–looking and highly effective arrangement.

A wide variety of cutters of all shapes and sizes is available in most good cake decorating shops, but is also possible to take an impression from a fresh leaf, as illustrated in the step–by–step pictures opposite.

Fresh foliage is not always available, however, and it is useful to have a supply of veiners. These are available commercially, but moulds can also be made at home, following the simple instructions on page 46.

On this page you will find instructions for making holly, ivy and carnation leaves. The embossing technique opposite is particularly suitable for rose, blackberry and violet leaves.

VARIEGATED HOLLY Two sizes of holly cutter, depicted right, are required for this leaf. Roll out a piece each of green and yellow flower paste on a lightly greased board. Place a length of 28 gauge wire on the yellow paste. Using the smaller cutter, cut out a small dark green holly leaf. Place this on top of the wire, sandwiching it between the yellow and green paste. Use a dowel to roll the edge of the leaf as thinly as possible, avoiding the wire. Cut out the holly using the larger cutter to give a yellow edge to the leaf. Shape and smooth the edge of the leaf with a bone tool. Allow it to dry before dusting it with dusting powder (petal dust/blossom tint) and varnishing with confectioners' glaze, see page 46.

VARIEGATED IVY Using the appropriate cutter and cream coloured paste, cut an ivy leaf. Wire

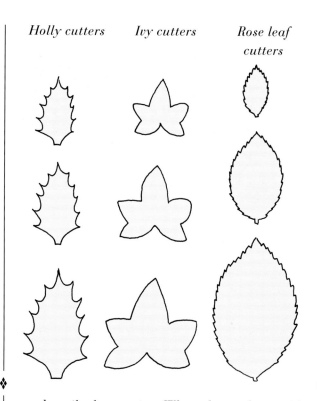

Holly cutters   *Ivy cutters*   *Rose leaf cutters*

as described opposite. When dry, colour with dusting powder (petal dust/blossom tint): brush several shades of green and yellow from the wire out to the edge of the leaf, leaving some parts cream. For extra effect a brush with a small amount of liquid colouring can be dabbed on the edges required to be darkest. When dry, hold the leaf over the steam of a boiling kettle to set the colour and give a slight gloss, see page 46.

CARNATION Roll some blue/green paste into a small sausage shape. Insert a 26 gauge wire through the centre. Use a dowel to roll and elongate the paste. Mark a line down the centre. Pinch the tip of the leaf to a point, then leave to dry slightly curved. Dust bottom and tip of leaf with yellow dusting powder (petal dust/blossom tint). Spray with fat to glaze, see page 46.

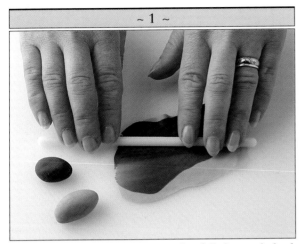

~ 1 ~

LEAVES Roll out a piece each of light and dark green flower paste on a lightly greased board. With dark paste on top of light, roll each side of paste as thinly as possible, leaving a slightly thicker strip down the middle.

~ 2 ~

Rub the back of a fresh rose, blackberry or violet leaf with white vegetable fat. Centre leaf on paste and apply gentle pressure, then use a scalpel to cut around shape of leaf. Remove fresh leaf to reveal veining on flower paste leaf.

~ 3 ~

Holding flower paste leaf between finger and thumb, insert a 26 gauge wire into central thicker part of leaf. Smooth edge of leaf with a bone tool. Create natural-looking movement by twisting the leaf slightly, then leave to dry.

~ 4 ~

Colour leaf with dusting powder, using a 2cm (³/₄ in) brush and working from edge of leaf towards middle. Leaves can be glazed in various ways to achieve realistic looking foliage, see page 46.

VEINING

There are many types of leaf veiner on the market, but it is quite easy to make your own moulds, using modelling clay and latex. Both these items are available from art and craft suppliers. It is important to choose non–toxic products.

Find a suitable leaf with good vein structure. Knead some modelling clay until pliable, then roll it out thinly. Press leaf into clay. Leaving a 5mm ($^1/_4$ in) border all around leaf, trim off excess clay. Roll a clay rope to make a small wall around edge of leaf. Leave clay to harden or bake, following manufacturer's instructions.

Paint a layer of latex over surface of mould and allow to dry for 30 minutes. Pour latex into mould. Leave overnight to dry. Liquid will become opaque when set. The latex mould can now be pulled away from the clay, ready for use.

GLAZING

The natural gloss on some flowers, leaves and berries can be imitated by careful glazing.

STEAMING Steam from a boiling kettle can be used to glaze flowers or foliage. Allow the flower paste leaves or flowers to dry completely, then dust with dusting powder (petal dust/blossom tint). Pass the flowers or leaves briefly through the steam – just long enough to give the paste a gloss; the flower or leaf should not be soaking wet or the paste could disintegrate. Allow to dry. Repeat the process if a higher gloss is required. An advantage of this method is that the steam will set the dusting powder and prevent the colours

from marking the cake surface, but care must be taken as steam can seriously scald the skin.

VARNISH Confectioners' varnish is a non–toxic glaze which is particularly useful for holly leaves and blackberries. The painted leaves or berries are dipped into the liquid, which will then dry to a high gloss. Confectioners' varnish is easy to use, but any brushes used will need to be cleaned with a non–toxic solvent.

FAT The liquid fat available in aerosol cans is very useful for glazing foliage. Colour leaves with dusting powder (petal dust/blossom tint) and place them on absorbent kitchen paper. Hold can about 20cm (8 in) from leaves; spray lightly. Allow leaves to dry overnight. The high gloss visible on the leaves when wet will have dulled to leave a realistic glossy surface. The benefit of using spray is that dusting powder or painted colour is not disturbed by brushing the leaf.

ROSES

Roses are always popular, whether as tiny buds, wild blooms such as Nazomi or full blown flowers like the exquisite open roses on page 49.

Flower paste is perfect for the delicate petals, and by combining flowers of various sizes and maturity – including one or two stamens whose petals have 'dropped' – you can create an arrangement so realistic that few who see it will believe the flowers are not freshly picked from a cottage garden.

COLOURING FLOWER PASTE FOR ROSES

Colour a small amount of paste (the size will depend on the number of roses needed) to the deepest colour required. Several different colourings can be added to the flower paste to achieve the desired hue. When satisfied with the colour, cut the paste in half. Place one half in a polythene bag and mix the rest with an equal quantity of white paste. Once again, put half in a polythene bag, and mix the rest with an equal amount of white paste. Put this in a third polythene bag. Keep all paste covered in polythene until required.

To give depth to the rose centre, use the deepest colour first. The petals should gradually become paler as the rose opens.

Step–by–step instructions for making roses are on page 48–49.

Rose petal cutters

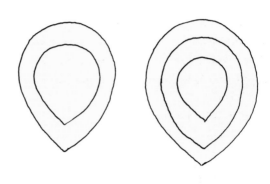

Calyx cutters

~ 1 ~

ROSE Roll a small piece of darkest paste into a ball. Thread a hooked wire through paste, then shape paste into a cone. Using a cocktail stick, roll one side of cone to a flag shape. Brush with egg white; wrap flag tightly around cone.

~ 2 ~

Cut 2 petals from darkest paste. Frill edges and cup centres. Brush egg white on 'V' of petal; attach to bud so top of petal is level with bud. Tuck second petal into first to form a spiral. Add 2 more petals, this time in medium colour.

~ 3 ~

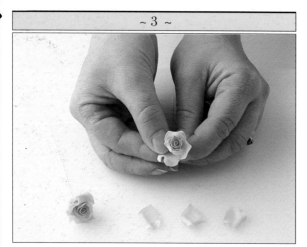

Cut 3 petals from medium paste. Using a cocktail stick, curl back opposite corners on 2 petals and both corners of third. Brush 'V's with egg white. Overlap curled edges of 2 petals on rose. Cup third petal around back.

~ 4 ~

Sandwich dark green paste on top of light green paste. Roll out thinly and cut out calyx. Make tiny cuts into edge; cup with ball tool. Brush centre with egg white. Thread calyx on wire. Attach a small ball of paste on back of dry rose.

~ 1 ~

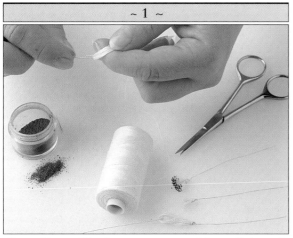

OPEN ROSE *Wind cream cotton (thread) loosely around index finger. Twist 28 gauge wire tightly through loops. Remove cotton. Twist second piece of wire through other end. Cut loops to make 2 sets of stamens. Wire upright. Dip ends in fat, then in brown cornmeal.*

~ 2 ~

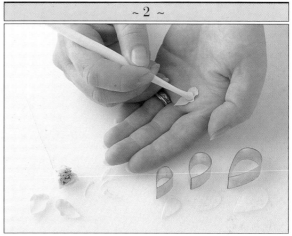

*Colour 3 pieces of paste different shades. Using darkest shade and smallest cutter, cut out 7 petals. Smooth and slightly frill edges; cup centres. Cut one petal into 3 strips, secure petals to stamens with egg white. **NOTE** For cutters, see page 47.*

~ 3 ~

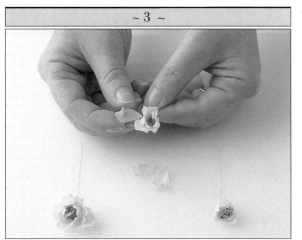

Using medium coloured paste and medium size cutter, cut 6 petals; repeat with light paste and large cutter. Paint 'V's with egg white. With flower upside down, attach petals in rows of 3.

~ 4 ~

When rose has dried, make a calyx using the pulled cutter method, see page 26. Cup sepals by stroking back of calyx from point to centre with a bone tool. Brush egg white in centre; push calyx onto rose wire.

TIERED WEDDING CAKE

15 x 10cm (6 x 4 in) oval cake
20 x 15cm (8 x 6 in) oval cake
25 x 20cm (10 x 8 in) oval cake
apricot glaze
3kg (6½ lb) marzipan (almond paste)
clear alcohol (gin or vodka)
4kg (8¾ lb) sugarpaste
Royal Icing, see page 8
Flower Paste for posy holders, see page 8
EQUIPMENT
23 x 18cm (9 x 7 in) oval cake board
28 x 23cm (11 x 9 in) oval cake board
33 x 28cm (13 x 11 in) oval cake board
scriber
no. 2 and 1 piping tubes (tips)
small paintbrushes
3 posy holders
white ribbon to trim boards
perspex (plexiglass) cake stand
FLOWERS AND LEAVES
(ASSORTED SIZES)
100 leaves, see page 45; 7 rose buds, see page 48; 10 half roses, see page 48; 7 open roses, see page 49; 6 rosehips, see page 49

● The cakes are shaped in the same way as the Christening Cake illustrated on page 15. On a sheet of paper, draw around tins (pans) used to bake cakes. Reposition tins over front edge and draw a matching arc on each circle. Cut out templates and use to trim cakes to required shape. Reserve templates; they will be required later for the top of each cake.

● Brush cakes with apricot glaze and coat with marzipan (almond paste). Leave to dry. Brush cakes with alcohol. Cover cakes and boards separately with white sugarpaste. Allow to dry for three days. Secure coated cakes to boards.

● Measure height and circumference of each cake, excluding curved front. Make a greaseproof paper (parchment) template for each cake. Fold paper into six equal sections. Trace appropriate embroidery design, see page 71, on each section of template, ensuring that all pencil lines are on one side of paper only. Attach a template to each cake, pinning ends. Scribe each cake design; remove templates.

● Pipe a small shell border around base of each cake with a no.2 tube (tip) and white royal icing. Brush embroidery is used for larger petals on side design of each cake. Use a no.1 tube and white royal icing to pipe brush - embroidered petals, brushing each one with a damp paintbrush as it is piped, see Note. Using same tube, pipe remaining petals with a zig–zag action. Change to a no.0 tube and pipe scalloped base borders and stems. Dry.

● Top each cake with the paper template; using a no.1 tube (tip) and white royal icing, outline templates with small S– and C– scrolls.

● Make flowers and leaves into sprays, see page 61. A close-up photograph of a spray is on page 4. Insert a small posy holder into the centre front of each cake to accommodate the wires of each spray. Place a small piece of flower paste inside each holder so that as flowers are put into place paste sets and holds them in position. Trim boards with ribbon. Display on a perspex (plexiglass) tube stand.

NOTE Detailed instructions for brush embroidery are not included in this book as the technique is covered elsewhere in the *Sugarcraft Skills* Series.

LILY

A large specimen bloom such as a lily can be made by studying the makeup and shape of a real flower. Begin by sketching the way the petals overlap, then carefully pull the flower apart, drawing around the petals on a piece of card. Number the petals in order as they are removed from the flower so that the paste petals can be put together in precisely the same fashion. The lily opposite was made in this way. Sketches of the essential petals appear right. Before you begin, make card templates for the inner and outer petals. One of the features of a lily is its distinctive stamens. To replicate these, cut the bottom and top off a stiff stamen. Roll a tiny piece of paste to a boat shape and thread it onto the stamen. Make 6 stamens in this way. When dry, dip the stamens into paprika coloured dusting powder (petal dust/blossom tint). Attach stamens to stigma following Step 1 opposite.

The petals are made in the same way as the leaves on page 45: roll out some white paste so that it is thicker down the centre than at the sides. Place the cardboard template on the paste and cut it out accurately, using a scalpel. Make 3 inner and 3 outer petals. Insert a 26 gauge wire into the thickest part of each petal (as for leaves). Finish making the flower following Steps 2–4.

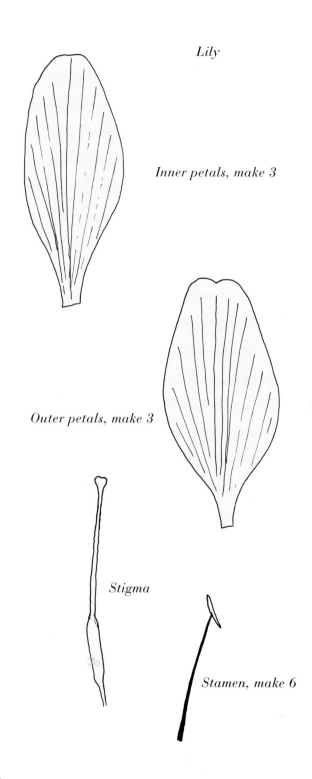

Lily

Inner petals, make 3

Outer petals, make 3

Stigma

Stamen, make 6

~ 1 ~

LILY To make the stigma, work a small ball of white paste onto the tip of a 24 gauge wire. Using tweezers, pinch the paste three times so that it resembles a clover in shape, see sketch left. Attach stamens to stigma with green floristry tape.

~ 2 ~

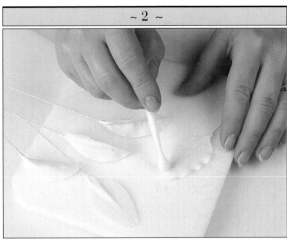

Smooth edge of each petal with a bone tool, texture it with a veiner, then leave to dry, slightly curving back tips of petals to create a natural–looking effect.

~ 3 ~

Colour front and back of each petal with dusting powder. Brush a line of green down centre, add a strip of yellow on either side of green line, then brush orange dusting powder from petal edge to centre.

~ 4 ~

Steam glaze petals, see page 46. When dry, tape 3 inner petals to stigma wire, surrounding stamens. Then tape outer petals, positioning them between the first petals to form a six–sided flower.

PINE CONES AND BERRIES

*C*ones and berries look extremely effective in a winter spray of foliage, and have been used on the Christmas Cake on page 57.

CONES Chrysanthemum flower cutters, illustrated right, are used to make the body of the cone. Begin by cutting two flowers in each size. The shape of the cone is built up gradually. To start with, only a 3 petal section of the smallest flower shape is used. For the next layer, a 4–petal section is wrapped around the cone just below the first. By increasing the number and size of petals progressively a realistic-looking cone is produced, see Steps 1–3 opposite. When the cones are dry, they can be glazed or painted with gold colouring, if liked.

BERRIES These are very easy to make. Add some black food colouring to red flower paste, making several different shades through to burgundy. Taking a ball of paste the size of a small pea, thread through the centre a black stamen; the stamen head should just show in the tip of the berry. Shape the paste into a slightly oval shape. Allow the berries to dry, then varnish following Step 4 opposite.

Chrysanthemum cutters, also used for pine cones.

- 1 ~

CONES *Thread a ball of brown paste onto a 24 gauge hooked wire. Shape into a 1cm (¹/₂ in) cone; allow to dry. Cup petals on smallest flower. Cut off 3-petal section, brush with egg white; wrap around point of cone. Repeat with 4-petal section.*

~ 2 ~

Cup petals on next size flower, stroking from outer edge to centre. Cut off 5–petal section. Cut small 'V' in base so petals can be stretched around cone. Repeat, using 6–petal section. Continue until all cut flower shapes are used.

~ 3 ~

Cut out one more flower in each size. Indent each petal with veining tool. Paint egg white on centre of each flower in turn and stick them together as shown. Brush egg white on back of cone; thread back petals in place.

~ 4 ~

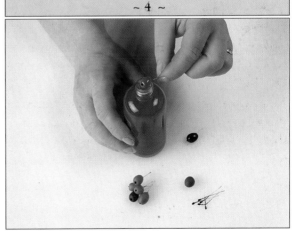

BERRIES *Having made berries as described opposite, dip into varnish; dry on wax paper. For extra shine, dip berries in varnish again. Tape stamens of berries to a 26 gauge wire.*

SEASONS GREETINGS

25 x 20cm (10 x 8 in) oval cake
apricot glaze
1.25kg (2½ lb) marzipan (almond paste)
clear alcohol (gin or vodka)
1.5kg (3 lb) sugarpaste
Royal Icing, see page 8
red, green and gold food colourings
yellow dusting powder (petal dust/blossom tint)

E Q U I P M E N T
33 x 28cm (13 x 11 in) oval board
no. 1 tube (tip)
2m (2 yd 6 in) red ribbon with gold line,
3mm (⅛ in) wide
scalpel
1cm (½ in) round cutter
3m (3½ yd) striped ribbon, 15mm (5/8 in) wide
1.5m (4¾ ft) ribbon to trim board

F L O W E R S   A N D   F O L I A G E
18 holly leaves, see page 44; 22 ivy leaves,
see page 44; 35 berries, see pages 54–55;
6 gold–painted cones, see pages 54–55

Cut a small arc from the front of the cake. Brush cake with apricot glaze and cover with marzipan (almond paste). Brush with alcohol; coat cake and board separately with white sugarpaste. Dry for 3 days.

Place cake on coated board. Trace inscription (page 70) on greaseproof paper (parchment) and scribe on cake. Using a no.1 tube (tip) and white royal icing, pressure pipe inscription. When dry, carefully paint lettering with gold food colouring.

The candles on the side on the cake incorporate ribbon insertion. Cut a strip of paper to go around side of cake. Fold it in half lengthwise to mark centre line, then fold paper in half widthwise to find centre back of cake. Mark 6 pencil points on lengthwise fold at 5cm (2 in) intervals on either side of centre back, making 13 pencil points in all. (Candles are not put around front of cake as they would be obscured by flower spray.)

Place pattern around cake and make a pin hole 5mm (¼ in) above and below each pencil point to indicate position of ribbon pieces. Remove paper pattern. Cut 13 ribbon pieces, each 1cm (½ in) long, from red and gold ribbon. Make a small cut with a scalpel and insert ribbon pieces, see Note. Place small round cutter above each ribbon insertion in turn and dust inside with yellow dusting powder (petal dust/blossom tint). Using sketch on page 70 as a guide, pipe a shell for the flame, using yellow royal icing and a no.1 tube (tip). When dry, paint centre of each flame orange. Pipe holly and berries with a no.1 tube and suitably coloured royal icing.

Attach striped ribbon to base of cake with royal icing, making join at front indent. Trim board with ribbon. Wire holly, ivy, berries and cones into sprays, following instructions on page 61, and including ribbon loops made from remaining ribbon if liked. Cut stem wires on sprays as short as possible and attach to cake with royal icing, taking care not to allow any wires to penetrate coating.

NOTE Detailed instructions for ribbon insertion are not included in this book as the technique is covered elsewhere in the *Sugarcraft Skills Series*.

ORCHID

*O*rchids are formal flowers which are traditionally associated with special occasions. They look effective, and are not difficult to make. Start by making card templates of the throat and petals on this page, then make the flower, following Steps 1–3 opposite. When the throat and petals are dry, add colour as follows: brush lemon dusting powder (petal dust/blossom tint) along the centre of each petal and inside the orchid throat. Paint the spots on the lip. Carefully dust each petal and the throat with lilac or pink dusting powder, working from the edge to the centre. Assemble the orchid following the instructions in Step 4.

Orchid templates

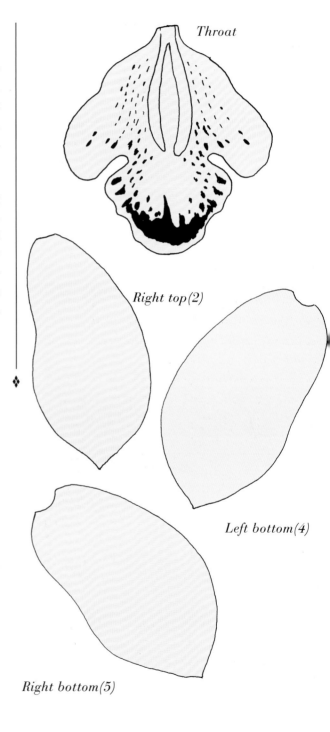

Throat

Right top(2)

Left bottom(4)

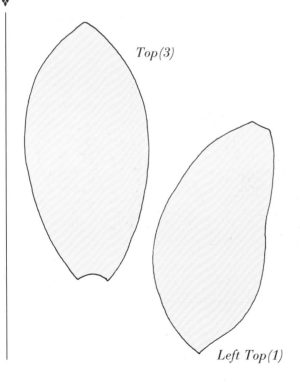

Top(3)

Right bottom(5)

Left Top(1)

~ 1 ~

ORCHID *Insert a hooked 24 gauge wire through a pea–sized ball of paste until the hook is buried. Shape paste into a 2.5cm (1 in) cone. Hollow one side with bone tool. Make a small semicircular cut in top of paste; curve slightly and dry.*

~ 2 ~

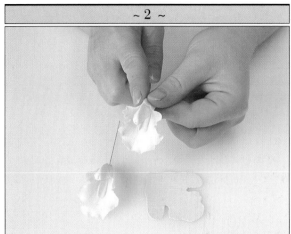

Using card template, cut throat from white paste. Place small rope of yellow paste along centre; divide in half with veining tool. Frill edge of lip using bone tool. Paint egg white on 'V' of throat; secure to prepared wire.

~ 3 ~

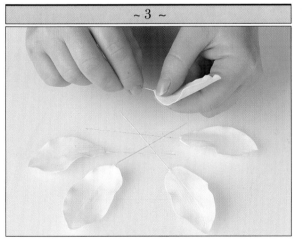

When orchid throat is dry, cut out the 5 petals, using appropriate templates. Wire each petal, following leaf method described on page 45. Shape petals and allow to dry.

~ 4 ~

Having coloured throat and petals, secure green floristry tape as close to orchid throat as possible. Attach top petals (1,2 & 3). Now tape bottom petals (4 & 5) as close to throat as possible. The petals can be moved gently close to wire where paste is thicker.

SPRAYS, BOUQUETS AND POSIES

*M*aking beautiful flowers, leaves and berries is an art in itself, but it is only the first step for the dedicated cake decorator. How the flowers are used – as deceptively simple sprays assembled directly on the cake surface; as posies, carefully balanced for all round viewing; or as bouquets shaped to complement the design of the cake – is a skill that takes time and patience to master. Take a tip or two from your favourite florist; study bridal bouquets or flower arrangements that are particularly attractive, and select colours with care, perhaps using the colour circle on page 39 for inspiration. Balance is extremely important; flowers should enhance the cake, not overwhelm it, so careful planning is a must. Step–by–step instructions for making a posy are given on page 34. This basic shape can be turned into a teardrop, crescent or S–shape by making one or two separate sprays and binding them to the posy. Bouquet returns are described in detail on pages 64–65.

POSY HOLDERS

To prevent the wires from the flowers penetrating the coating on the cake, several types of holder are available. A small core of icing, marzipan and cake should be removed and the holder gently pushed into the cake. A small piece of soft flower paste can be placed in the holder to secure the bouquet and prevent accidental damage in transit. The use of posy holders is illustrated right.

POSY HOLDERS can be used straight or at an angle on the top, side or corner of a cake. This photograph shows the use of a small posy holder for the sweet pea spray used on the 18th Birthday Cake on page 42.

The posy holder should protrude slightly above the cake surface so that it may be seen and removed by the person cutting the cake. This holder is used on the Ruby Wedding Cake on page 66.

~ 1 ~

DIRECT FLOWER SPRAY *Make a selection of flowers. Draw shape of spray on paper. Tape flowers together with floristry tape, frequently matching spray against pattern (2 identical sprays are used here). Set some single blooms aside.*

~ 2 ~

Secure a small piece of sugarpaste to cake or plaque (in this case a bible made from sugarpaste and flower paste) with egg white. Push wires of sprays firmly into the soft paste.

~ 3 ~

Place another piece of sugarpaste over wires. Cut wires of single blooms to required length and gently push them into the sugarpaste.

~ 4 ~

Continue building up shape of spray with single flowers. Tweezers are very useful for inserting flowers which are close together. Wires must never penetrate cake coating.

CORSAGE

$\mathcal{U}$nlike the exquisite S-shaped spray opposite, in which full blown roses, rose buds, carnations, daisies and a variety of other blooms have been used to create a fluid and fairly informal S-shaped bouquet, the corsage is dominated by two large orchids.

Step-by-step instructions for making the orchids are on page 59. They are combined with 18 sprays of blossom (pages 11 and 61) and 15 pulled flowers with cotton centres (page 12).

To make the spray, tape blossom and pulled flowers in groups of three with floristry tape. Bind the orchids together with a long length of reel wire. Carefully wire the sprays of flowers to either side of the orchids, adding 3 ribbon loops (page 16), if liked. The spray should measure about 25cm (10 in) in length. Tape the wire stems with white floristry tape.

NOTE The rose spray opposite is made by binding two returns to a posy, see pages 64–65.

EXPERT ADVICE

≈

If the corsage is to be used on a cake covered with royal icing, be careful not to crack the icing when inserting the posy holder. The best way to make a hole in royal icing is to use a sharp pointed knife, turning the tip gently in circles to drill through the coating.

~ 1 ~

BOUQUET RETURNS *Adding separate sprays to a posy can create a variety of shapes. Begin by making a pattern for the return: draw a circle the same size as the posy, then draw a triangle from the edge of the circle the length of the required return.*

~ 2 ~

Cut a piece of white floristry tape in half lengthwise. Begin taping smaller flowers together, matching the bouquet against the design to obtain the correct shape. Stretch the floristry tape as you bind the flowers; it will stick when stretched.

~ 3 ~

Continue taping the flowers together, remembering that the arrangement should have height as well as breadth. The central height of the return should be equal to its width.

~ 4 ~

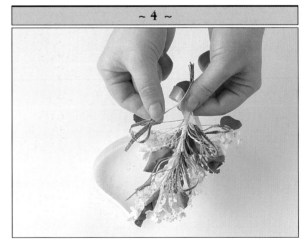

Tape two or three ribbon loops to the back of the return to help to mask the binding, and also to continue the colour theme throughout the spray. Bind the return to the posy, following the step–by–step instructions opposite.

~ 1 ~

TEARDROP BOUQUET WITH RETURN *Make a posy following step–by–step instructions on page 34. Do not cut the reel wire or tape the stem of the flowers. Using matching flowers, make a bouquet return of the required length, see Steps 1–4 opposite.*

~ 2 ~

Hold bouquet return against posy. Look to see where wires cross at the back. Mark the wires. Now bend the return stem to a 90° angle at the marked point. The flowers of the posy and return should now appear to be one piece.

~ 3 ~

Bind the bouquet together with the reel wire. Cut the stem to the required length and tape with white floristry tape.

NOTE *This bouquet is used on the Ruby Wedding Cake illustrated on page 67.*

~ 4 ~

A crescent or S–shaped bouquet is formed by wiring another return to the opposite side of the bouquet. Gently curve the bouquet into the required shape with your hand. See also photograph on page 63.

RUBY WEDDING CAKE

13cm (5 in) diameter bell–shaped cake
30 x 25cm (12 x 10 in) oval cake
apricot glaze
2kg (4 lb) marzipan (almond paste)
clear alcohol (gin or vodka)
2kg (4 lb) sugarpaste
Royal Icing, see page 8
silver food colouring

EQUIPMENT

15cm (6 in) round board
38 x 33cm (15 x 13 in) oval board
scriber
3m (3¼ yd) scarlet ribbon, 3mm (⅛ in) wide
Garrett frill cutter
cocktail stick (toothpick)
paintbrushes
no.1 and 0 piping tubes (tips)
dividers
scalpel
large posy holder
small silver wine bottle coaster

FLOWERS

5 scarlet rose buds; 5 scarlet half roses and 1
scarlet full rose, see pages 48–49;
10 cream freesias, see page 31; 17 lemon filler
carnations, see page 27; 10 sprays white
blossom, see page 11; 20 rose leaves,
see page 45; 10 pulled flowers, see page 12;
and 12 sprays dried gysophilia

● Brush cakes with apricot glaze and cover with marzipan (almond paste). Brush with clear alcohol and coat with sugarpaste. Dry for three days; attach each cake to board. Measure height and circumference of oval cake and make a paper template. Fold template into 8 equal sections, attach to side of cake and mark each section with a pin hole. Scribe a line around base of both cakes 4cm (1½ in) above board. Attach ribbon to base of each cake.

● Using cutter, white sugarpaste and cocktail stick (toothpick), make Garrett frills. Moisten scribed line on each cake with a damp brush and quickly attach frills, see Note, page 36. When applying frills to oval cake, leave a clear space on right side for flower spray. Make two layers of frills and neaten top edge with a herringbone shell using a no.1 tube (tip) and white royal icing. Use same tube to pipe embroidery on oval cake between marked divisions; for template, see page 69.

● Make a greaseproof paper (parchment) template for ribbon insertion on oval cake. Except where it curves inward, template should be same shape as cake and 10cm (4 in) smaller. Position template and mark spaces for ribbon insertion with dividers set at 1cm (½ in). Use ribbon insertion template on page 69 for bell cake. Cut pieces of scarlet ribbon slightly longer than divisions. Use a scalpel to make small cuts in sugarpaste coating, then insert ribbon, see Note, page 56. Using a no.0 piping tube (tip) and white icing pipe embroidery between each piece of ribbon. Use same tube for inscription. When dry, paint lettering with silver food colouring.

● Make teardrop spray for top of bell cake, see pages 64–65. The spray on the oval cake board is made by wiring a small return, see page 64.

● Insert posy holder in bell-shaped cake. Before positioning bouquet, pipe numerals on side of bell using white royal icing and a no. 0 tube (tip). When dry, paint with food colouring. Assemble cakes, using silver coaster to separate tiers.

TEMPLATES

Easter Cake, page 36

Side design
Daffodil   *Violet*   *Daffodil*

Birthday Cake, page 24

Bluebird, make 1

Happy Birthday

Figure for plaque

Runout teddies, make 4

Runout plaque

40

Ribbon insertion template

Ruby Wedding Cake, page 66

Congratulations

Side motif Ruby Wedding Cake, page 66

Engagement Cake, page 32

Wings

Birds

Hollow heart plaque

Oval plaque

Side template

18th Birthday Cake, page 42

With Love

Seasons Greetings Cake, page 56

Numeral for cake. Enlarge to size req

Seasons Greetings

Dusting powder

Ribbon insertion

Wedding Cake, page 50

Brush embroidery

Scalloped edge

INDEX

FOR FURTHER INFORMATION
Merehurst is the leading publisher of cake decorating books and has an excellent range of books to suit cake decorators of all levels.
Please send for a free catalogue, stating the title of this book:–

United Kingdom
Marketing Department
Merehurst Ltd.
Ferry House
51–57 Lacy Road
London SW15 1PR
Tel: 081 780 1177
Fax: 081 780 1714

U.S.A/Canada
Foxwood International Ltd.
P.O. Box 267
145 Queen Street S.
Mississauga, Ontario
L5M 2BS Canada
Tel: (1) 416 567 4800
Fax: (1) 416 567 4681

Australia
J.B. Fairfax Ltd.
80 McLachlan Avenue
Rushcutters Bay
NSW 2011
Tel: (61) 2 361 6366
Fax: (61) 2 360 6262

Other Territories
For further information
contact:
International Sales
Department at United
Kingdom address.